THE NORDIC REGION

DENMARK

KATIE GILLESPIE

AV2

www.openlightbox.com

Step 1
Go to **www.openlightbox.com**

Step 2
Enter this unique code
SRLWVFM3S

Step 3
Explore your interactive eBook!

AV2 is optimized for use on any device

Your interactive eBook comes with...

Contents
Browse a live contents page to easily navigate through resources

Audio
Listen to sections of the book read aloud

Videos
Watch informative video clips

Weblinks
Gain additional information for research

Slideshows
View images and captions

Try This!
Complete activities and hands-on experiments

Key Words
Study vocabulary, and complete a matching word activity

Quizzes
Test your knowledge

Share
Share titles within your Learning Management System (LMS) or Library Circulation System

Citation
Create bibliographical references following APA, CMOS, and MLA styles

This title is part of our AV2 digital subscription

1-Year 3–8 Subscription
ISBN 978-1-7911-3306-1

Access hundreds of AV2 titles with our digital subscription.
Sign up for a FREE trial at **www.openlightbox.com/trial**

The digital components of this book are guaranteed to stay active for at least five years from the date of publication.

THE NORDIC REGION

DENMARK

Contents

AV2 Book Code 2
Denmark Overview 4
Exploring Denmark 6
Land and Climate 8
Plants and Animals 10
Natural Resources 11
Tourism 12
Industry 14
Goods and Services 15
Early Inhabitants 16
The Vikings 17
A Dramatic History 18
Population 20
Politics and Government 21
Cultural Groups 22
Arts and Entertainment 24
Sports 26
Mapping Denmark 28
See What You Have Learned 30
Key Words 31
Index 31

Denmark Overview

Denmark is the most southerly of the **Nordic countries**. Along with Sweden and Norway, it is part of a northern European region called Scandinavia. Denmark's people, known as Danes, enjoy a high standard of living. Denmark ranks above many other nations in health, education, jobs, housing, social connections, and environmental quality. The country is consistently rated one of the best places in the world to live.

Focus on Denmark

Capital
Copenhagen

Population
5.9 million

Currency
Danish krone

National Coat of Arms

National Flag

National Anthems
"Kong Kristian stod ved højen mast"
("King Christian stood by the lofty mast")

"Der er et yndigt land"
("There is a lovely land")

National Animal
Mute Swan

National Flower
Marguerite Daisy

National Butterfly
Small Tortoiseshell

Exploring Denmark

Denmark has an area of 16,580 square miles (42,942 square kilometers). Jutland occupies more than two-thirds of the country's land area. This **peninsula** is located north of Germany. Denmark also has more than 400 islands. Located east of Jutland, they are called the Danish **archipelago**. Denmark is surrounded by the North Sea and Baltic Sea. It shares maritime borders with several countries, including Poland, Sweden, and Norway.

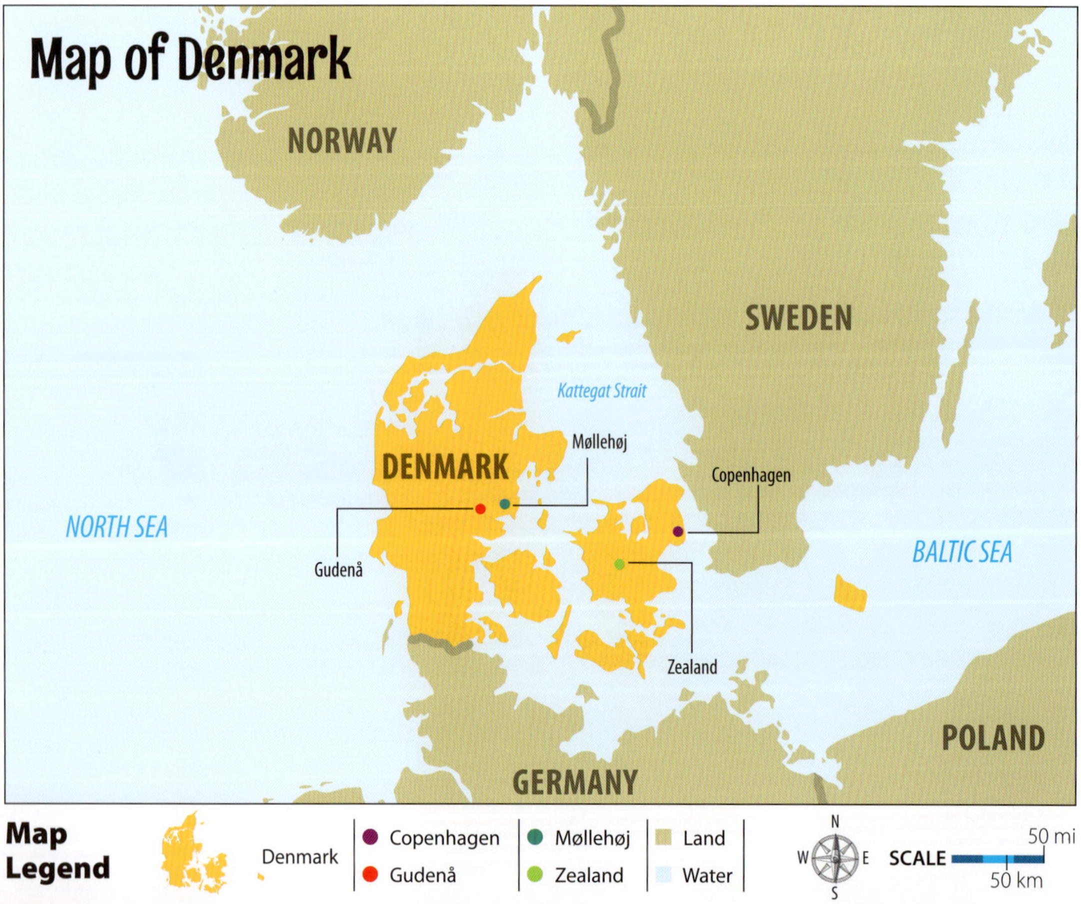

Copenhagen

Copenhagen is Denmark's largest city. It became the country's capital in 1445. Today, Copenhagen is known for its rich history and impressive modern architecture. It is a popular tourist destination.

Zealand

Covering 2,715 square miles (7,032 sq. km), Zealand is Denmark's largest island. It is between the Baltic Sea and Kattegat Strait. Zealand features **urban** settlements, beaches, and ancient castles.

Møllehøj

Møllehøj is the highest natural point in Denmark. It has an **elevation** of 561 feet (171 meters). Located in eastern Jutland, Møllehøj is part of the Ejerbjerge hills.

Gudenå

The Gudenå is Denmark's longest river. It extends 98 miles (158 km) in length. The river begins in east-central Jutland. It flows toward the coast and empties into Randers **Fjord**.

Land and Climate

Denmark is a small country. Its entire area is less than twice that of Massachusetts. Denmark extends about 250 miles (402 km) north to south and 220 miles (354 km) east to west. The terrain is mostly low and flat. The average elevation is only 100 feet (30 m) above sea level. Denmark's coastline measures more than 4,500 miles (7,242 km). It features a variety of **inlets**, lagoons, and gulfs. No part of the country is more than 30 miles (48 km) from the sea.

The country has five first-level administrative regions. These are North Denmark, Central Denmark, South Denmark, Zealand, and the Capital Region. They are further divided into 98 second-level units called municipalities.

Denmark has a **temperate** climate. Its weather is heavily influenced by the country's proximity to the sea and the European continent. Wind direction, ocean **currents**, and the seasons also affect Denmark's weather.

Denmark's coastline features several unique rock formations. Bornholm Island is home to the *Helligdomsklipperne*, or "Sanctuary Rocks," a series of jagged cliffs and rock pillars that soar up to 72 feet (22 meters) in height.

Since the country is small and flat, there is little variation in climate between Denmark's regions. However, Jutland's west coast, which faces the North Sea, tends to be rainier and windier than the rest of the country. Days are dark and short from October to March. Half the yearly sunshine occurs from May to August. Denmark's longest days are recorded in June.

Denmark's winters are generally mild. Average temperatures are just above freezing in January and February. Summers are pleasant, with average temperatures ranging from 60 to 64° Fahrenheit (16 to 18° Celsius) in July and August. Spring is cool and dry. Autumn is rainy and windy.

Annual precipitation averages about 25 inches (64 centimeters). This ranges from about 16 inches (41 cm) in the archipelago to 32 inches (81 cm) in southwestern Jutland. There are typically 20 to 25 days of snow between November and April.

Seasonal Denmark

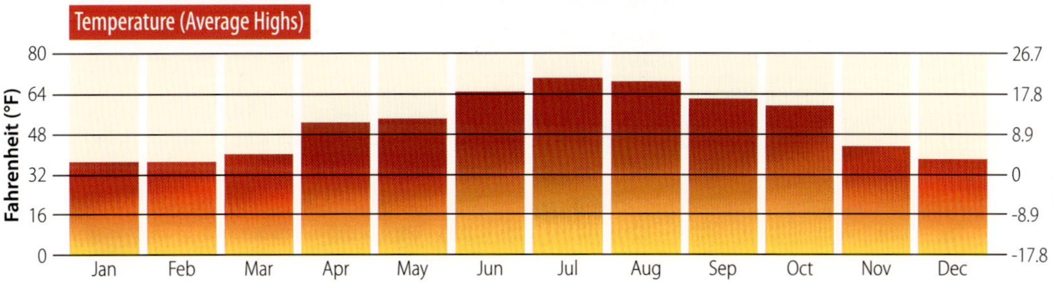

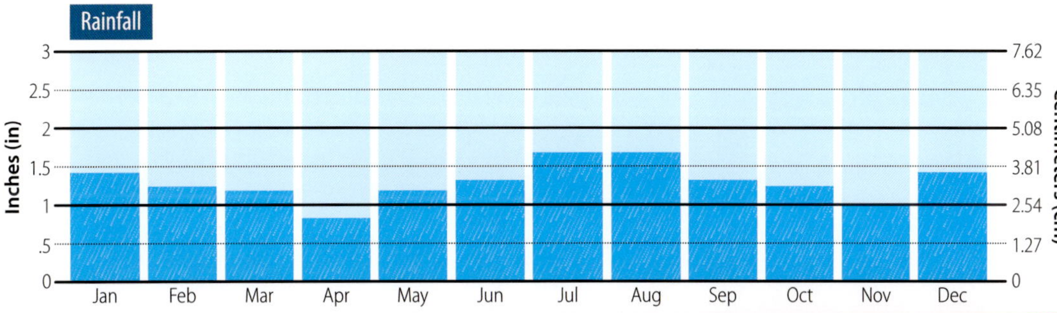

Plants and Animals

Within the dense forests of Rold Skov lies Store Blaakilde, a spring known for its sapphire-blue waters.

About 30,000 **species** of plants and animals live in Denmark. The country was once covered by **deciduous** trees. Today, due to land development, only about 16 percent of Denmark is forested. These forests are mainly **coniferous**. The most common tree is the Norway spruce. Jutland's Rold Skov is the country's largest forest. In addition to spruce, it features many different fir and pine trees.

Several species of deer, including red, fallow, and sika, live in Denmark. The smallest is the roe deer. These agile animals stand only 24 to 33 inches (61 to 84 cm) high at the shoulder. They weigh 33 to 66 pounds (15 to 30 kilograms).

Denmark is also home to more than 300 bird species. About two-thirds of these species breed in the country. The rest **migrate** to warmer areas. A variety of fish live in Denmark's waters. They include herring, cod, flatfish, sea trout, garfish, and pike. Denmark is also known for its wide variety of butterflies.

The red deer is Denmark's largest land mammal. Males can measure more than 4 feet (1.2 m) high at the shoulder and weigh up to 530 pounds (240 kg).

The moor frog is one of several frog species found in Denmark. Besides moors, it can be found in and around lakes and other wetland areas.

Natural Resources

Denmark produces limestone for both domestic and international markets.

Denmark possesses limited natural resources. However, those it does have are valuable. Several of the country's natural resources help support the energy, health, and construction sectors.

Danish waters in the North Sea contain crude oil and natural gas. These reserves are large enough to make the country self-sufficient in both resources. About 2.6 billion gallons (9.8 billion liters) of crude oil are extracted from Danish waters every year. Both it and the country's natural gas are used to produce heat and electricity for homes and businesses throughout Europe. Denmark has a variety of renewable energy sources as well. These green alternatives include water, wind, and solar power.

Denmark's underground resources provide materials for a variety of industries. Salt is extracted for use in health products. Clay, chalk, limestone, **moler**, sand, and gravel are all necessary for the building industry. These resources can be used to make bricks, tiles, cement, or insulating materials.

Located south of Copenhagen, the Avedore power station is one of the world's most energy-efficient heat and power plants. Using a combination of oil, natural gas, wood pellets, and straw, it is able to provide heat to more than 200,000 homes and electricity for up to 600,000 households.

Tourism

Denmark is the smallest Scandinavian country. Despite this, it has the largest tourism market in the region. In 2020, more than 15 million tourists visited Denmark. They spent more than $9 billion.

One of the country's most famous residents was Hans Christian Andersen. Born in 1805, this storyteller is world-renowned for his fairy tales. They are still widely read today. Visitors to Andersen's hometown of Odense can explore his childhood home, as well as a museum devoted to his life's work. Another popular tourist attraction related to the author can be found in Copenhagen. Located at Langelinie Pier is a bronze statue called *The Little Mermaid*. It depicts the title character from one of Andersen's best-known stories.

Visitors to Rosenborg Castle can view King Christian IV's crown. Dating back to 1596, it is the oldest crown in the royal collection.

Copenhagen is also home to Tivoli Gardens. Tivoli is one of the world's oldest amusement parks. It has delighted guests since 1843. In addition to extensive flower gardens, Tivoli features a variety of dining options and live entertainment. It also has rides, such as its famous wooden roller coaster.

Denmark's castles draw tourists from around the globe. Some of the most remarkable castles can be found in Copenhagen. Amalienborg Palace is the residence of the Danish Royal Family. The Crown Jewels and Royal **Regalia** are kept at Rosenborg Castle. Christiansborg Palace houses the Danish Parliament and Supreme Court.

Tivoli Gardens has approximately 30 rides for guests to enjoy, as well as a plethora of shops and restaurants.

Travelers interested in science will enjoy Copenhagen's Round Tower. Constructed in the early 17th century, the tower is Europe's oldest functioning **observatory**. It was built to continue the research of Danish astronomer Tycho Brahe. A **planetarium** named after the scientist is another popular attraction. It features a variety of exhibitions, along with IMAX and 3D films.

Denmark has museums to suit a variety of interests. The country is well known for its **Viking** history. At the Viking Ship Museum in Roskilde, visitors can explore a hall where five original Viking ships are displayed. History buffs can also enjoy the Museum of National History and the National Museum of Denmark. Art lovers often make time to visit the National Gallery of Denmark. Located in Copenhagen, it has the largest art collection in the country, with some works dating back about 700 years.

Industry

Among the many products manufactured in Denmark are LEGO building bricks, popular children's toys. The LEGO company was founded in Denmark in 1932.

Denmark has a **gross domestic product (GDP)** of nearly $400 billion. This comes mainly from service industries, trade and transport, and manufacturing. The majority of Danish workers are employed in these sectors.

Manufacturing, mining and quarrying, and utility services provide jobs for more than 330,000 Danes. Danish companies manufacture a variety of products. These include medications, machinery, and transport equipment. Food processing is also a large part of the manufacturing industry.

Fishing, forestry, and agriculture make only a small contribution to Denmark's GDP. However, they are still important to the country. About 42,000 people are employed in these sectors. Denmark's annual **fish landings** total approximately 700,000 tons (635,000 metric tons). Most of this catch is comprised of cod, herring, and flatfish.

Grains grow in more than half of the nation's farmland. The most common are wheat and barley. Other major crops include potatoes, turnips, and sugar beets. Farmers also raise cattle, pigs, poultry, foxes, and minks.

Denmark GDP by Sector

The combined value of Denmark's top three sectors accounts for more than half of the country's total GDP. All other sectors range from about 1 to 10 percent each.

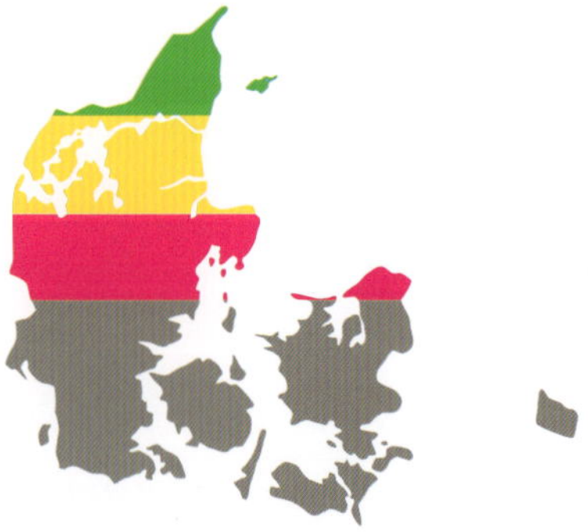

20.93%
Public Administration, Education, and Health

19.73%
Trade and Transport

15.04%
Manufacturing

Goods and Services

Copenhagen Airport is Denmark's largest international airport. Its more than 2,300 employees serve approximately 9 million passengers annually.

The majority of Danes are employed in the public administration sector. This includes service jobs in fields such as education and healthcare. Tourism is another growing service sector. However, it is mostly seasonal.

Denmark's economy relies on trade with other countries. Each year, it **exports** more than $100 billion in goods and services. The country's main exports include meat, cheese, medications, and machinery.

Several products are **imported** into the country as well. Among the top imports are cars, computers, and smartphones. Denmark also imports refined petroleum. This can be used as fuel for transportation, heating, and generating electricity.

In 1973, Denmark became the first Nordic country to join the European Economic Community (EEC). The EEC was later succeeded by the **European Union (EU)**. As an EU member, Denmark depends on foreign trade within Europe. Some of Denmark's key trading partners are Germany, the Netherlands, Norway, Sweden, and the United Kingdom.

Many of the goods entering and leaving Denmark travel by ship. The city of Aarhus is home to the country's largest container port. It handles approximately 11 million tons (10 million metric tons) of cargo per year.

Early Inhabitants

The growth of agriculture in Denmark brought the creation of pottery, as people needed containers for crop storage. The Skarpsalling pot was found in northern Denmark in 1891. It dates back to about 3200 BC.

People have lived in the area now known as Denmark since the end of the last **Ice Age**. These first inhabitants arrived from southern and eastern Europe in about 10,000 BC. They were hardy explorers who survived by hunting and fishing. Most of their tools and weapons were made of stone. As nomads, these people moved often, likely following herds of reindeer.

By 4000 BC, agriculture had been introduced to Denmark. Farmers cleared land for villages, planted fields of crops, and kept livestock. In approximately 1800 BC, stone tools were replaced by bronze. These were followed by iron tools in about 500 BC. Over time, a more structured society, with established farming practices and religious rituals, began to emerge.

By 200 AD, the Danes were trading with the Romans. This relationship is believed to have led to the development of a written Danish language, in the form of **runes**. The population was devastated by the **bubonic plague** in the 6th century. However, Danish society was able to recover and flourish. By the 8th century, the first major trading centers had formed at Hedeby and Ribe.

The island of Mon is known for prehistoric monuments called menhirs, or bauta stones. Typically found near burial mounds, they are believed to serve as memorials to the dead.

The Vikings

The Vikings built vessels ranging from small fishing boats to longships. The largest of the Viking warships were called drakkars.

During the 9th century, the Vikings came to power. They included not only people from Denmark, but also Sweden, Norway, and later Iceland. Today, many think of the Vikings mainly as violent raiders. However, there is more to this group than raiding and pillaging.

In addition to their many conquests, the Vikings traveled to other nations to trade. They were skilled at building and sailing ships. This gave them an advantage when it came to conquering by sea and fueled their fearsome reputation. Their extensive travels took them far and wide. They ranged north of the Arctic Circle, south to Africa, west to North America, and east to Russia.

Perhaps the best-known Danish Viking was King Harald I. Also called Bluetooth, he is renowned for unifying the country in the 10th century. Harald brought **Christianity** to Denmark as well. This eventually led, in part, to the end of the Viking era in the 11th century.

Besides being warriors and traders, most Vikings were also farmers. Their farms were often small, and the family lived with their animals in a home called a longhouse.

A Dramatic History

In 1397, Denmark was united with Sweden and Norway, along with their territories, including Greenland, Iceland, and the Faroe Islands. This historic achievement was known as the Kalmar Union. It was led by a sole ruler, Queen Margrethe I. She was the first official Danish **head of state**.

The Kalmar Union ended in 1523, when Sweden gained its independence. This marked the beginning of a long rivalry between Denmark and Sweden. Several wars were fought between the two countries.

As Denmark and Sweden fought for dominance in the region, Denmark and Norway remained united. One of their most famous kings was Christian IV. Crowned in 1596, he ruled Denmark and Norway for six decades. Christian was responsible for founding several new towns. He also built castles and other structures in and around Copenhagen.

Even after the Thirty Years' War, Christian IV continued to fight for dominance in northern Europe. When threatened by Sweden in 1643, he went to sea to defend his territory, losing an eye in battle. Ultimately, Sweden won the fight, and Christian was forced to cede land to his enemy.

Against the advice of his councillors, Christian entered the **Thirty Years' War**. This attempt to make Denmark the leading nation of the region was unsuccessful. More wars followed, and Sweden started to take over as the dominant Nordic power. In the early 19th century, the **Napoleonic Wars** spread to Denmark. This led to the defeat of the Danish Navy by the British. By 1814, with the signing of the Treaty of Kiel, Denmark had ceded Norway to Sweden. Thirty-five years later, Denmark adopted a new constitution, paving the way for the country to become a **democratic** nation.

Denmark held a neutral position in both world wars. However, the country was occupied by Germany in 1940, during **World War II**. Despite Denmark's neutral status, Danish resistance groups were formed to help fight the Germans.

In 1944, Iceland declared its independence from Denmark. It broke all political ties to Denmark and became a **republic**. With the loss of Iceland, the country was reduced to its current size.

The German occupation of Denmark began on April 9, 1940, and lasted until May 4, 1945, just days before the war in Europe came to an end.

Population

Denmark is home to approximately 5.9 million people. Its population is steadily increasing. The population is projected to be above 6 million by 2030. Of all the Nordic countries, Denmark is the most densely populated. It has about 380 people per square mile (147 people per square km). This is four times as much as the United States, which has a population density of about 94 people per square mile (36 people per sq. km).

Denmark consistently ranks as one of the happiest countries in the world. In 2022, it placed second, behind Finland.

Approximately 88 percent of Denmark's people live in urban areas. Copenhagen has a population of about 645,000. More than 1.3 million people live in its metropolitan area. The second largest city is Aarhus, with about 350,000 people. Odense and Aalborg are the only other Danish cities with populations above 100,000.

The median age in Denmark is about 42 years. Life expectancy is approximately 80 years. Danish women generally live slightly longer than men.

Denmark Age Groups

Nearly two-thirds of Denmark's population is between 15 and 64 years old. Those above and below this range are split fairly evenly, with a slightly higher senior population.

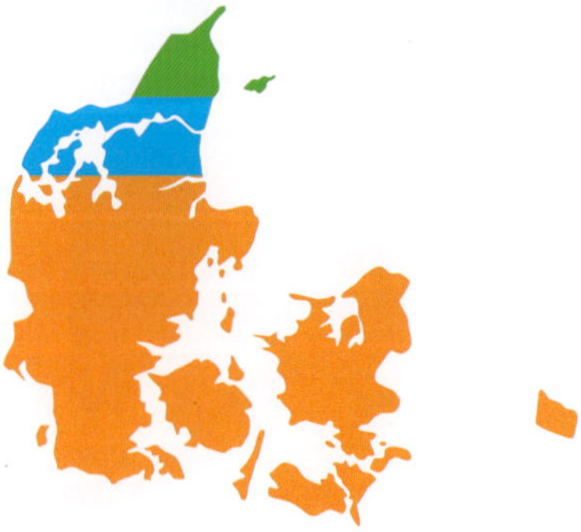

16.4%

Age 0–14 years

63.3%

Age 15–64 years

20.3%

Age 65+ years

Politics and Government

Denmark is a constitutional monarchy. In this system, there is a monarch, or individual ruler. The monarch is the official head of state. However, this role is largely ceremonial, with limited political power. Denmark's current monarch is Queen Margrethe II. Her main tasks are to represent the country abroad and be a **figurehead** at home.

Denmark is also a parliamentary democracy. Members of the Danish parliament, or Folketing, are elected to their positions. Elections take place every four years. Members from multiple parties come together to form a **coalition**. The leader of one of the strongest parties becomes the prime minister.

The fundamental principles that rule Danish society are set by the Constitutional Act of Denmark. The act also lays out how the country is to be governed, dividing power between three independent branches. The Folketing is the legislative power. It passes the country's laws. The government is the executive power. This branch makes sure that laws are carried out. The law courts are the judicial power. They pass judgments in disputes.

The Folketing is made up of 179 members of Parliament. The majority, 175, are elected in Denmark, but Greenland and the Faroe Islands, both Danish dependencies, have two representatives each.

Queen Margrethe II has been Denmark's ruler since 1972. She is Europe's longest-serving living monarch and its only reigning queen.

Cultural Groups

Most of Denmark's inhabitants are of Danish descent. This means having one or both parents born in Denmark, and possessing Danish citizenship. However, the country also has several minority groups. These include Germans, Swedes, Norwegians, Turks, Poles, Iraqis, Bosniaks, Iranians, and Somalis. Although Greenlanders and Faroese have Danish citizenship, few of them actually live in continental Denmark.

Danish, or Dansk, is Denmark's official language. It is spoken by more than 5 million people. These speakers are found not only in the country, but in some communities across the German border. Danish is also spoken in Iceland, Greenland, and the Faroe Islands. About 86 percent of Danes are bilingual. Most speak English as their second language. Other languages are spoken by different ethnic groups. These include Arabic, Turkish, Swedish, and German.

Most street signs in Denmark use only the Danish language. English translations may appear on signs in areas where tourists are common.

The vast majority of Danes are Christian. Roman Catholicism was Denmark's official religion until 1536, when it was replaced by another branch of Christianity called Lutheranism. Today, nearly 75 percent of Danes belong to the state church. Called the Evangelical Lutheran Church of Denmark, it is also known as the *Dansk Folkekirke*, or the Danish People's Church.

Considered the religious center of Denmark, Copenhagen has some of the country's grandest churches. Frederik's Church is known for its majestic copper dome, which provides visitors with sweeping views of the city.

The largest non-Christian faith in Denmark is Islam, with approximately 270,000 followers. People have practiced Judaism in the country for more than 400 years, but the Jewish community is quite small today. About 0.4 percent of the population follow Hinduism. Another 0.2 percent practice Buddhism. Almost 19 percent of Denmark's residents are not affiliated with any religion.

Arts and Entertainment

People from many artistic disciplines hail from Denmark. Several of Denmark's entertainers have achieved worldwide recognition. These include writers, actresses, actors, filmmakers, and musicians.

Three Danes have been awarded the Nobel Prize in Literature. Henrik Pontoppidan and Karl Adolph Gjellerup shared the prize in 1917. Johannes Vilhelm Jensen won it in 1944. Another Dane, Karen Blixen, was nominated twice. She is best known for her memoir, *Out of Africa*.

Many talented actresses come from Denmark as well. Brigitte Nielsen has appeared in two films in the long-running *Rocky* series, *Rocky IV* and *Creed II*. Connie Nielsen is recognized for her role in the blockbuster film *Gladiator*. She can also be seen in many popular DC movies, including *Wonder Woman* and *Justice League*. Amanda Collin stars on the HBO series *Raised by Wolves*.

Denmark has produced its fair share of accomplished actors, too. Mads Mikkelsen has been part of several large film franchises. Among his credits are the James Bond film *Casino Royale*, Marvel Studios' *Doctor Strange*, and the Star Wars spin-off *Rogue One*. Most recently, he starred in the 2022 film *Fantastic Beasts: The Secrets of Dumbledore*. His older brother Lars Mikkelsen is also a successful actor. He was featured on the acclaimed BBC series *Sherlock* and the animated series *Star Wars Rebels*. Danes Nikolaj Coster-Waldau and Pilou Asbæk are known for their work on the massive hit show *Game of Thrones*. Giancarlo Esposito, from the Star Wars series *The Mandalorian*, was born in Copenhagen.

Connie Nielsen portrayed the character of Hippolyta in *Wonder Woman* and its sequel, *Wonder Woman 1984*. Hippolyta is the mother of Diana Prince, also known as Wonder Woman.

Since its founding in 1981, Metallica has played in stadiums across the globe and sold more than 150 million albums worldwide.

Danes are also known for their musical abilities. Carl August Nielsen was a classical composer who conducted the Copenhagen Musical Society. His *Maskarade,* created in 1906, is often referred to as Denmark's national opera. As co-founder of the band Metallica, drummer Lars Ulrich is one of Denmark's best-known modern musicians. He and his bandmates were inducted into the Rock and Roll Hall of Fame in 2009.

Sports

Whether they participate themselves or act as spectators, Danes enjoy a variety of sports. Denmark is known for its professional athletes. Many have achieved greatness in competitions around the world.

Soccer, or football as it is called in Denmark, has been the country's most popular sport since the 1870s. A number of successful football players come from Denmark. Some of the best known are Christian Eriksen, Kasper Schmeichel, Yussuf Poulsen, Kasper Dolberg, Andreas Christensen, and Simon Kjær.

In 2022, Denmark qualified to play in its sixth FIFA World Cup. For only the second time in its history, the team was eliminated before the knockout round, losing to Australia 1–0.

Denmark has also produced several talented tennis players, including Torben Ulrich and Kenneth Carlsen. Denmark's top rated tennis star is Caroline Wozniacki from Odense. She turned pro at just 15 years of age. Over her career, from 2005 to 2020, Wozniacki won 30 singles titles. She was the first Scandinavian woman to reach the top-ranking singles position. She held that ranking for 71 weeks.

Roskilde's Kevin Magnussen is a well known Formula One racecar driver. He drove for the McLaren team in the 2014 FIA Formula One World Championship. Currently, he is a driver for Haas Racing. Motorsports run in his family. His father Jan Magnussen was also a racing driver, with four Le Mans GT class wins.

Camille Rasmussen is a young gymnast from Copenhagen. In 2022, her performance at the Challenge Cup earned her a historic silver medal, making her the first female gymnast from Denmark to win a World Cup or Challenge Cup medal. Rasmussen also earned silver at the 2022 Nordic Championships.

Over the course of her tennis career, Caroline Wozniacki earned more than $35 million in prize money.

Denmark has a rich Olympic history as well. It has participated in every Olympic Games except one. Over the years, the country's Olympians have had some amazing accomplishments. Swimmer Inge Sørensen from Skovshoved was only 12 years old when she won a bronze medal in the 200-meter breaststroke at the 1936 Summer Olympics. She set a record as the youngest Olympic medal winner in an individual competition. More recently, badminton player Viktor Axelsen won gold for his singles performance at the 2020 Summer Olympics. It was the first ever win by a European player.

Mapping Denmark

We use many tools to interpret maps and to understand the locations of features such as cities, states, lakes, and rivers. The map below has many tools to help interpret information on the map of Denmark.

Denmark Map

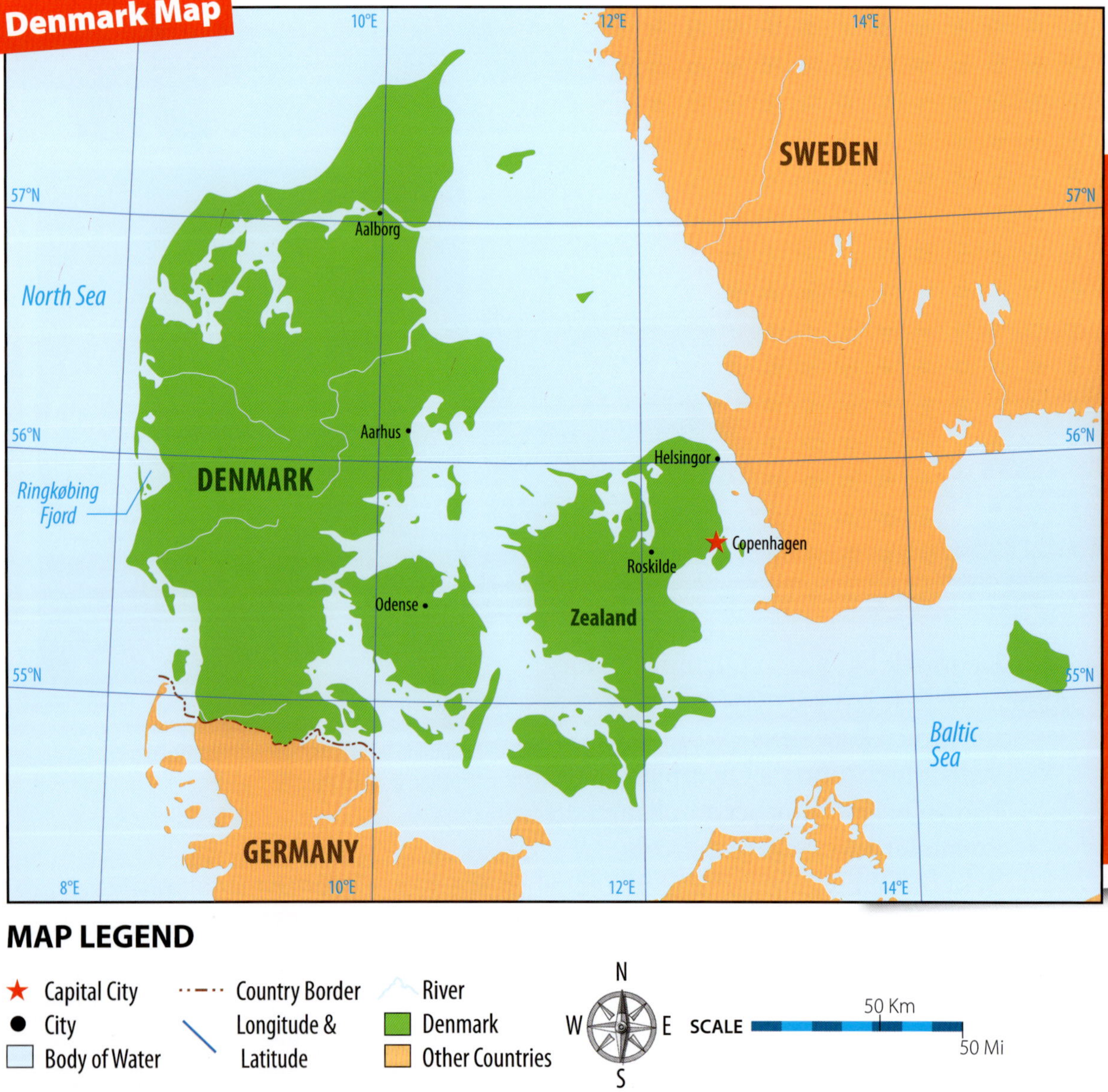

Mapping Tools

- The compass rose shows north, south, east, and west. The points in-between represent northeast, northwest, southeast, and southwest.
- The map scale shows that the distances on a map represent much longer distances in real life. If you measure the distance between objects on a map, you can use the map scale to calculate the actual distance in miles or kilometers between those two points.
- The lines of latitude and longitude are long lines that appear on maps. The lines of latitude run east to west and measure how far north or south of the equator a place is located. The lines of longitude run north to south and measure how far east or west of the Prime Meridian a place is located. A location on a map can be found by using the two numbers where latitude and longitude meet. This number is called a coordinate and is written using degrees and direction. For example, the city of Copenhagen would be found near 55°N and 12°E on a map.

Map It!

Using the map and the appropriate tools, complete the activities below.

Locating with latitude and longitude

1. Which island is located at 55°N and 12°E?
2. Which inland body of water is located near 56°N and 8°E?
3. Which city is located near 56°N and 10°E?

Distances between points

4. Using the map scale and a ruler, calculate the approximate distance between Aalborg and Aarhus.
5. Using the map scale and a ruler, calculate the approximate distance between Roskilde and Odense.
6. Using the map scale and a ruler, calculate the approximate distance between Helsingor and Copenhagen.

ANSWERS 1. Zealand 2. Ringkøbing Fjord 3. Aarhus 4. 59 miles (95 km) 5. 68 miles (110 km) 6. 25 miles (40 km)

See What You Have Learned

Test your knowledge of Denmark by answering these questions.

1 In what year did Iceland declare its independence from Denmark?

2 Which city was Hans Christian Andersen from?

3 What is the national flower of Denmark?

4 When did the Vikings come to power?

5 How many species of plants and animals live in Denmark?

6 What is the population density of Denmark?

7 What is Denmark's GDP?

8 How many islands does Denmark have?

9 What is the most popular sport in Denmark?

10 What does the Folketing do?

ANSWERS

1. 1944
2. Odense
3. Marguerite daisy
4. During the 9th century
5. About 30,000
6. About 380 people per square mile (147 people per square km)
7. Nearly $400 billion
8. More than 400
9. Soccer, or football
10. Passes the country's laws

Key Words

archipelago: a group of islands
bubonic plague: a serious bacterial infection that is often fatal
Christianity: the religion based on the teachings of Jesus Christ
coalition: a group formed when different political parties come together for a particular purpose
coniferous: trees that produce cones
currents: steadily moving water
deciduous: trees that lose their leaves in autumn and grow new leaves in spring
democratic: pertaining to the principle of rule by the people
elevation: the height of an area of land above sea level
European Union (EU): a political and economic organization, established in 1993, that has more than two dozen member countries
exports: sells goods to other countries
figurehead: a person in a leadership position who does not have any real power
fish landings: the catches of marine fish landed in ports
fjord: a narrow body of water that reaches inland
gross domestic product (GDP): the total value of goods and services produced in a country or area
head of state: the main representative of a country
Ice Age: a long period of time when Earth's climate was especially cold
imported: bought goods from other countries
inlets: narrow bodies of water that cut into a coastline
migrate: travel to another place when the season changes
moler: a marine rock deposit found in Denmark that is used for insulation, cement, or other purposes
Napoleonic Wars: a series of wars between the French Empire and other European powers that took place in the 1800s and 1810s
Nordic countries: a group of countries in northern Europe, consisting of Denmark, Finland, Iceland, Norway, and Sweden
observatory: a structure that holds a large telescope for observing the stars and planets
peninsula: an area of land mostly surrounded by water
planetarium: a theater devoted to education and entertainment in space science
regalia: emblems of royalty, such as a crown or scepter
republic: a form of government in which a state is ruled by representatives of the people
runes: characters of ancient Norse alphabets
species: a group of living things with similar attributes
temperate: mild or moderate
Thirty Years' War: a 17th-century conflict fought in central Europe
urban: related to cities and towns
Viking: a Scandinavian seafaring warrior who raided Europe between the 9th and 11th centuries
World War II: a war that lasted from 1939 to 1945, involving many of the world's countries

Index

Aarhus 15, 20, 28, 29
Andersen, Hans Christian 12, 30

Baltic Sea 6, 7, 28
Brahe, Tycho 13

castles 7, 12, 18
Christian IV 12, 18
climate 8
Copenhagen 5, 6, 7, 11, 12, 13, 15, 18, 20, 23, 24, 25, 26, 28, 29

European Economic Community (EEC) 15
European Union (EU) 15

Faroe Islands 18, 21, 22
Folketing 21, 30

Germany 6, 15, 18, 28
Greenland 18, 21, 22
Gudenå 6, 7

Harald I 17

Iceland 17, 18, 22, 30

Jutland 6, 7, 8, 10

Kalmar Union 18

languages 16, 22

manufacturing 14
Margrethe I 18
Margrethe II 21
mining 14
Møllehøj 6, 7
monarchy 21
museums 12, 13

Napoleonic Wars 18
Netherlands 15
North Sea 6, 8, 11, 28

Odense 12, 20, 26, 28, 29, 30
Olympics 27

plants 10, 30

religion 22, 23
Rold Skov 10
Roskilde 13, 26, 28, 29

Thirty Years' War 18
Tivoli Gardens 12, 13
tourism 7, 12, 13, 15, 22

Vikings 13, 17, 30

World War II 18

Zealand 6, 7, 8, 28, 29

Published by Lightbox Learning Inc.
276 5th Avenue, Suite 704 #917
New York, NY 10001
Website: www.openlightbox.com

Library of Congress Control Number: 2022951634

ISBN 978-1-7911-4718-1 (hardcover)
ISBN 978-1-7911-4719-8 (softcover)
ISBN 978-1-7911-4720-4 (multi-user eBook)

Printed in Guangzhou, China
1 2 3 4 5 6 7 8 9 0 27 26 25 24 23

022023
101322

Project Coordinator Heather Kissock
Designer Terry Paulhus

Photo Credits
Every reasonable effort has been made to trace ownership and to obtain permission to reprint copyright material. The publisher would be pleased to have any errors or omissions brought to its attention so that they may be corrected in subsequent printings. The publisher acknowledges Getty Images, Alamy, Newscom, Bridgeman Images, Shutterstock, Dreamstime, and Wikimedia as its primary image suppliers for this title.